Summary Contents

I0011090

978168 1090412

TABLE OF CONTENTS

ABBREVIATIONS

A	Grantee (for present estate/ future interest hypotheticals)
AGI	Adjusted gross income
AP	Adverse possession
B	Buyer
C	Constitution
CIF	Cause-in-fact
Cl.	Clause
CLEO	State Chief Law Enforcement Officer
Court (cap.)	United States Supreme Court
CP	Court of Pleas (UK)
CR	Contingent remainder
CSD	Common Scheme of Development
CSI	Compelling state interest
Ct.	Court
Ct. App.	Court of Appeals
Ct. Chan.	Court of Chancery (England)
ED	Emotional distress
EI	Executory interest
Eng.	England
ES	Equitable Servitude
FLSA	Fair Labor Standards Act
FMLA	Family and Medical Leave Act
FQJ	Federal question jurisdiction
FRAP	Federal Rules of Appellate Procedure
FRCP	Federal Rules of Civil Procedure
FRCrP	Federal Rules of Criminal Procedure
FRE	Federal Rules of Evidence
FS	Fee simple absolute (fee simple)
FSCS	Fee simple on condition subsequent
FSD	Fee simple determinable
FS EL	Fee simple on executory limitation
FT	Fee tail
H.L.	House of Lords (England)
JMOL	Judgment as a matter of law
JNOV	Judgment non obstante veredicto
JT	Joint tenant/tenancy
K	Knowledge (criminal law) or Contract (all other law)
K.B.	King's Bench (UK)
L	Loss in value
L1	First landlord
Lat.	Latin
LE	Life estate

LED	Life estate determinable
LLC	Limited liability company
LLP	Limited liability partnership
LRM	Least restrictive means
MPC	Model Penal Code
MSAJ	Motion to set aside the judgment
N.B.	Nota bene
O	Original owner, or grantor (in present estates and future interests)
P	Purpose or purchaser
PJ	Personal jurisdiction
PJI	Pattern Criminal Jury Instruction
Q.B.	Queen's Bench (UK)
R	Recklessness
RAP	Rule against perpetuities
RC	Real Covenant
Restatement	Restatement (of Contracts, Torts, Judgments, etc.)
RFRA	Religious Freedom Restoration Act of 1993
RLUIPA	Religious Land Use and Institutionalized Persons Act
RPP	Reasonable prudent person
Rule	Federal Rule of Evidence or Federal Rule of Civil Procedure
§	Section
S	Sublessee or seller
S.Ct.	Supreme Court or U.S. Supreme Court Reporter
SJ	Summary judgment
SMJ	Subject matter jurisdiction
SP	Specific performance
T1	First tenant
TE	Tenant/tenancy by the entireties
UCC	Uniform Commercial Code
US	United States of America or United States Reports (compilation of U.S. Supreme Court opinions)
USC	United States Code
VR	Vested remainder
VR SD	Vested remainder subject to divestment

CHAPTER 1. LANDLORD / TENANT LAW

I. INTRODUCTION

A. Leasehold Estates

A leasehold estate is one where the possessor (tenant) has only possession, and full title (including possession) will spring back to the owner (landlord) at the conclusion of the leasehold estate.

In a freehold estate, in contrast, the possessor is the owner of the property (at least for a temporary period of time).

1. Historical origins

In feudal times, the king owned all of the land. Nobles that were loyal to him were able to use parts of the land. They then were able to parcel land out to serfs and peasants.

Today, this many-layered system of tenancy continues to exist. For example, in commercial shopping centers, sections of a store may be parceled out to merchants many times over.

Later, leaseholds were established as collateral for loans. The tenant would "lend" the landlord the money in exchange for the use of the land. Rather than pay the loan back with interest, the landlord would simply grant the tenant use of the land. Eventually, the law began to recognize leaseholds as interests in land in and of themselves.

B. Three Kinds of Leaseholds

1. Tenancy for Years

a. Characteristics

A tenancy for years is a discreet lease with a determined beginning and end date. If there is a provision clause in the lease, then a second, separate one-time renewal lease may be established.

When there is a renewal clause in the lease, it is evidence of a tenancy for years, since periodic tenancies and at-will tenancies require no renewal to continue.

b. How It Is Created

A tenancy for years is created formally; it requires a clear end date. The end date need not be explicitly expressed, if the expiration of the lease could be determined. The following clause, for example, would be sufficient: "the lease will begin on Jan 1, 2000 and will expire three years later."

According to some authorities, there must also be a set start date. Under the majority view, however, it does not need to be fixed. The clause "the lease begins when the construction has ended" would be sufficient.

Under the modern law Statute of Frauds, any lease for more than one year must be in writing to be enforced.

c. How It Is Terminated

A tenancy for years ends automatically at the end of the term. The lease may provide the possibility of renewal. In such a case, a court would allow the new lease. Except for when a provision of the original contract (lease) is illegal, unclear or for some other reason against public policy, the original contract controls all matters in the new lease.

2. Periodic Tenancy

a. Characteristics

A periodic tenancy is an indefinite lease. There is no need for renewal.

b. How It Is Created

A periodic tenancy may be created by the parties in an express agreement (*e.g.*, "This lease is from month-to-month."). In addition, it may be created by law.

If the parties attempt to create a tenancy for years, but a period is mentioned (*e.g.*, "rent will be paid each month") and no end date is determined, then a periodic tenancy is presumed.

c. How It Is Terminated

Either party may end a periodic tenancy with *proper notice* (unlike tenancies at will, which do not require proper notice). For periods of one or more years, six months of notice is usually required. For periods of less than one year, notice equal to one full period (generally measured by payment periods) is required.

Generally, notice of termination must be in writing and delivered.

> Example: the tenant rents from a landlord in a monthly periodic tenancy. The tenant gives notice to the landlord on July 15 that he wishes to leave. Until when must the tenant pay rent?
>
> Since the tenant must have one full month of rent paid before vacating, all of August must be paid before leaving. Thus, the tenant is responsible for rent up until August 31.

3. Tenancy at Will

a. *Characteristics*

A tenancy at will may be terminated at any time.

b. *How It Is Created*

It is usually created by operation of law; if a tenancy for years is attempted, but there is no clear end date and no basis for ascertaining a period, then a tenancy at will is presumed.

Examples of tenancies where there is no basis for ascertaining a period:

- The landlord agrees to allow his tenant to live on the property on the condition that the tenant keeps up the property and pays the taxes and insurance.
- The tenant is an employee-at-will of a landlord who furnishes a home as part of the compensation.

c. *How It Is Terminated*

Under the common law, a tenancy at will can be ended at any time. In the modern era, many state statutes protect tenants, by requiring, for example, at least ten days of notice prior to the landlord's termination of the tenancy.

II. DISCRIMINATORY PREFERENCES AND RELIGIOUS LIBERTY ISSUES

A. The Evolution of Regulations on Landlords

Under the common law, a landlord could select whichever tenants or purchasers he wanted for his housing or land. Later, statutes prohibited landlords or sellers from discriminating on the basis of race, color, religion, sex, familial status, age, handicap or national origin. One example of such a statute is the federal Fair Housing Act.

The Fair Housing Act prohibits:

- Discrimination on the basis of race, color, religion, sex, familial status, age, handicap or national origin for the basis of choosing a tenant or buyer; and
- The *publication* or *indication* of a preference as to any of the above categories in choosing a buyer or tenant.

The subjective intent of the owner or landlord is irrelevant; what is controlling is whether a reasonable person from one of the protected groups would interpret an indication as expressing a preference.

> *See Jancik v. Department of Housing and Urban Development* (7th Cir. 1995), where the Seventh Circuit held that the landlord violated the Fair Housing Act by indicating his preference for a "mature person," which a reasonable person would take to mean a middle-aged tenant without small children, thus violating the statute on familial status. He also violated the statute by saying that he did not want any teenagers and by inquiring as to race with a discriminatory purpose. Damages and an injunction were affirmed.

Many states have adopted stricter versions of this federal act. Massachusetts, for example, has adopted statutes that also prohibit discrimination on the basis of sexual orientation.

Regulations are usually more lax for the rental of rooms attached to the owner's abode (*e.g.*, a landlord may chose a tenant based on gender).

B. Modern Statutes and Religious Liberty

Many state and federal statutes prohibit familial status discrimination. Such statutes do not necessarily prohibit landlords from discriminating against unmarried cohabitants. *See State v. French* (Minn. 1990).

Since there is no federal law protecting against marital status discrimination, claims for marital status discrimination fall to the states, whose regulations vary widely.

- Most states have either: (i) not passed statutes prohibiting discrimination based on marital status; or (ii) passed legislation prohibiting discrimination based on marital status, but explicitly exclude unmarried couples from protection.
- Other states have passed legislation protecting against marital status discrimination, but not specifically protecting unmarried cohabitants.

III. TENANT'S RIGHTS AND REMEDIES

A. Introduction

A tenant has four basic rights:

- Legal possession;
- Actual possession;
- The covenant of quiet enjoyment / constructive eviction; and
- The implied warranty of habitability.

Furthermore, he has certain remedies if the lease violates housing regulations.

B. Legal Possession

All states recognize tenants' right to legal possession. The landlord must have title in order to enter into a lease.

C. Actual Possession

The landlord has a duty to deliver the actual possession of the premises to the tenant. This duty prevents *third parties*, such as holdover tenants, from preventing new tenants from taking actual possession of the rented property.

English (majority) rule*:* the *landlord has the duty of delivering the actual possession* of the property and of preventing third parties from interfering with it.

- Some states that have adopted the English rule apply it only to *residential*, not *commercial*, leases).
- In states that have adopted the English rule, the tenant's remedy for the landlord's failure to deliver actual possession is *expectation damages. See Adrian v. Rabinowitz* (N.J. 1936).

American (minority) rule: the *new tenant is responsible for obtaining possession* of the property and for evicting holdover tenants; the landlord is merely a title holder.

In states that have adopted the American rule, the tenant has no remedy for the landlord's failure to deliver actual possession.

D. The Covenant of Quiet Enjoyment and Constructive Eviction

The covenant of quiet enjoyment and constructive eviction deals with the tenant's *actual and constructive continued possession* of the property after delivery. It is implied in all states except NJ.

There are two kinds of violations:

1. Actual (Full or Partial) Eviction

a. Overview

There are two kinds of actual eviction:

- *Eviction for lack of title:* a third party with superior title evicts the tenant from the property.
- *Wrongful eviction:* the landlord evicts the tenant without cause.

The promises in a landlord-tenant relationship are independent from one another. Thus, even if a lease is violated by a landlord, the tenant is generally not relieved of the duty to pay rent. However, a violation of the covenant of quiet enjoyment is the exception. Thus, if a tenant is evicted from the property, he is excused of the duty to pay rent.

b. Full and Partial eviction

Full eviction applies when a tenant is evicted from *all* of the property. An eviction is partial when the tenant is evicted from only *part* of the property. In either case, the covenant of quiet enjoyment protects the tenant.

Since the lease is seen at common law as a transfer of *all* the property, *exclusion from any of the property* is seen to be an eviction. Thus, the *remedy for partial eviction is similar to that for full eviction*: the obligation to pay rent is entirely excused until the tenant's full possession is restored. *See Smith v. McEnany* (Mass. 1897).

However, the restatement and many states take a different approach: partial eviction proportionally reduces the rent that the tenant must pay, but he is still obligated to pay rent for the *portion of the land from which he has not been evicted.*

2. Constructive Eviction

Some violations of the lease may be so material that the tenant can be considered to have been *constructively evicted*, even if he continues to hold actual possession of the land.

The elements of constructive eviction are as follow:

-   A material breach of the lease;
-   That is chargeable to the landlord;
-   Of which the landlord is given notice;
-   With the opportunity to cure; and
-   The tenant vacates the premises after a reasonable time.

Violations of peace and quiet can constitute violations of the covenant of quiet enjoyment.

> Example: the landlord leases a store to one tenant who opens a bookstore. The landlord then leases adjacent space to a second tenant, who opens up a gym that is always playing loud music. If the music is so loud that it alienates all of the first tenant's clients, the first tenant may have a claim for constructive eviction.

Constructive eviction places a burden on the tenant to vacate the premises and then bring an action to *terminate the lease and the duty to pay.* The problem with this is that it is possible that the tenant vacate the premises, sue, and lose. He will then be required to pay the rent, even though he has vacated the premises.

3. Remedies for Violations of the Covenant of Quiet Enjoyment

At common law, the tenant is *excused of the duty to pay rent* (in some states, if it is a partial eviction, he may do so while remaining in possession of the property). In other states, the tenant is entitled to money damages.

E. The Implied Warranty of Habitability

Because of the problems involving constructive eviction, some states have recognized the *implied warranty of habitability*. This warranty makes it easier for the tenant to recover damages when the condition of the premises is so poor that the tenant is *virtually constructively evicted*, whether the eviction be partial or full. In a minority of jurisdictions, for commercial leases, some states recognize an "implied covenant of suitability" in place of an implied warranty of habitability.

The implied warranty of habitability makes it possible to *recover the damages* that one would have recovered for constructive eviction (as well as other remedies, see *infra.*), but without the requirement that the tenant vacate the premises.

The implied warranty of habitability is breached when there is:

- A violation of a housing standard that is based on either (i) local laws providing *standards*; (ii) statutes providing *specific terms*; or (iii) statutes providing *general terms* (as in New York).
- That is chargeable to the landlord;
- With notice given to the landlord; and
- A reasonable opportunity to cure is given to the landlord.

At common law, the only thing that justified not paying rent was the violation of the covenant of quiet enjoyment. It later came to be seen that some violations of the warranty of habitability could be so gross that the defendant could be considered to have been evicted.

When the warranty is violated, the tenant has several possible remedies:

- To move out and terminate lease;
- To abate the rent;
- To remain in possession of the property, pay rent, and sue for damages;
- To repair the property and recover the money spent; or
- To remain on the property and withhold the rent. *See Richard Barton Enterprises, Inc. v. Tsern* (Utah 1996). *N.B.*: many courts require the tenant to put the rent in escrow.

F. Illegal Leases

1. The Common Law

At common law, the landlord did not have the duty to maintain the property, unless specifically provided in the lease. However, he had a duty to *make the premises safe*. If he failed, the tenant still had the

duty to pay rent, based on the independence of covenants, but he could *recover damages*.

2. The Modern Law

Today, if a lease is invalid because of a housing law violation, the tenant's options include:

- Moving out of the apartment and asking that the courts declare the lease invalid, thereby absolving him of the duty to pay rent; or
- Remaining in the apartment and:
  - Asking a court to order the landlord to conform the apartment to housing laws;
  - Conforming the housing to local laws and asking the court to reward damages equal to the funds spent;
  - Remaining in the housing with an abatement of the rent equivalent to the difference in the value between what the tenant *bargained for* (property in conformity with the law) and what he *received* (property not in conformity with the law). This is the Restatement § 6.1 approach; or
  - Remaining in the housing rent-free (accepted in a few jurisdictions).

IV. DURATION OF THE TENANCY AND USE OF THE PREMISES

A. Duration of the Tenancy

1. The Holdover Tenant

A holdover tenant is one who **keeps possession of the property** beyond the expiration of the lease. Landlords have a choice as to whether to (i) declare holdover tenants to be **trespassers** (and thus evict them); or (ii) declare a **new periodic tenancy** (equal to the length of the previous term), and thus to charge them. They may do this within reasonable time.

The period between the end of a lease and the landlord's deciding as to whether he will declare the holdover tenant to be a trespasser or a periodic tenant is known as a **tenancy at sufferance**. In order for a landlord to declare a new tenancy and to charge a tenant for another

period, the holdover tenant must **voluntarily remain** on the premises. *See Commonwealth Building Corp. v. Hirschfield* (Ill. 1940).

2. The Right to the Extended Occupancy of Certain Housing

Normally, a landlord has the right to terminate the tenant's right of occupancy at the expiration of the lease. There are, however, exceptions when occupants are living in *federally subsidized housing*. In such situations, tenants are constitutionally entitled to occupancy for life. However, eviction may occur if there is good cause (*e.g.*, illegal drug use on the premises by the tenant).

Similarly, there are statutes that protect the rights of **mobile home owners**. Since the costs of relocating are relatively high compared to the cost of the mobile home, some states require park owners to extend leases of at least one-year.

There is also a law regulating **rental units** being converted into **condominiums**. The purpose of these regulations is to *protect tenants who would be unable to purchase a condominium*.

Finally, there is legislation, such as the Senior Citizens and Disabled Protected Tenancy Act, NJSA 2A:18-61.22 et seq., that protects the **rights of senior citizens and the disabled**. If rental housing is converted into condominiums, some tenants are allowed a *forty year protected tenancy period*. To qualify, one must be:

-   *Disabled* to the point of being unable to engage in gainful activity; or
-   A *senior citizen* of over sixty two years of age, or a widow of more than fifty years of age who was married to a spouse who was sixty two years of age; and
-   Must have lived in the unit continuously for at least one year.

When a landlord converts a housing unit to a condominium, he must inform the agency, which then contacts the tenants to inquire whether there is anyone *eligible for the protected status*.

B. Restrictions on the Uses of the Premises

The hallmark of a lease is the tenant's *unrestricted possession*. This does not, however, mean *unrestricted use*. The uses of the property may be implied by the law or restricted by the landlord. The following are the only *implied* restrictions on use:

- Waste;
- Illegal or immoral uses; and
- Misrepresentation on the part of the lessee.

The landlord may also impose restrictions. He may, for example, restrict which businesses may rent the premises (*e.g.*, to avoid competitors in a strip mall). In order for the landlord to restrict the tenant's use of the premises, one of following elements must be met:

- The intentions of the parties must be clear; or
- Explicit restrictive language must be present in the lease, such as, "the tenant is to use the premises only as a restaurant." *N.B.*: without the word "only," this phrase would be considered to be *permissive, not restrictive*.

C. The Duty of Continuous Operations

There is *no implied duty of continuous operations*, unless one of the following elements are met:

- The lease includes a *specific provision* requiring continuous use; or
- There is an *implied covenant of continued use* based on the lease's implicit language or other circumstances. *See Lippman v. Sears* (Cal. 1955).

To determine whether an implied covenant of continued use is applicable in a case, courts may implement a balancing test that looks to the following factors (*Thompson Dev., Inc. v. Kroger Co.*):

- Whether the lease contains an *inconsistent provision*;
- Whether the lease grants *free assignability* to a tenant;
- Whether the lease was *freely negotiated* by all the parties; and
- Whether the lease contains a *non-competition provision*.

When the *base rent is token or nonexistent*, but the share of the profits is substantial, a court could infer continued operation as being within the parties' intent. When there is a *substantial base rent*, courts usually will not recognize an implied covenant of continued use. *See Piggly Wiggly Southern, Inc. v. Heard* (Ga. 1991).

V. FIXTURES

A. Common Law

At common law, fixtures remained with the landlord of the property.

B. Modern Law

The traditional modern law view is that fixtures remain with the landlord, but if they are installed by the tenant, they could be taken by the tenant, as long as (i) their removal would not damage the property; and (ii) they were removed *before expiration of the lease*.

However, the *general modern law rule* allows fixtures to be removed by tenants if the removal would not damage the property, *even if it is done after the expiration of the lease*, as long as it is done before possession of the property is yielded. *See Handler v. Horns* (N.J. 1949).

VI. LESSOR'S REMEDIES AGAINST DEFAULTING TENANTS

A. Termination of the Lease

A landlord may terminate a lease against a tenant who (i) **fails to pay** rent; (ii) **wrongfully possesses** the premises after the right has terminated; or (iii) **abandons the premises** before the end of the lease.

However, landlords may not terminate leases for **immaterial breaches**. *See Foundation Development Corp. v. Loehmann's, Inc.* (Ariz. 1990).

B. Eviction

The general rule is that given adequate notice, month-to-month leases may be terminated at any time for *any reason whatsoever*.

> Exception: when allowing landlords to evict tenants jeopardizes a public policy. *See Edwards v. Habib* (D.C. Cir. 1968).

1. Retaliatory Eviction

Retaliatory eviction refers to a landlord's eviction of a tenant based on the tenant's invocation of a protected right, reporting of a housing code violation, or some other act relating to the property. There are three approaches to retaliatory eviction:

- **Restrictive approach**: a tenant may only use the retaliatory eviction defense when the following occurs:
  o The property violates housing standards;
  o The tenant reports this to the housing authority; and
  o Immediately afterwards, the landlord tries to evict the tenant.
- **Intermediate approach**: a tenant may use the retaliatory eviction defense when the landlord tries to evict the tenant for any action that the tenant takes that is *related to the property*, such as his joining of a tenants union.
- **Permissive approach**: tenant may use the retaliatory eviction defense for an eviction resulting from tenant's exercise of *any legal or constitutional right*.

C. Damages

Expectation damages are awarded for the breach of a lease. If the tenant leaves the property prematurely and stops paying rent, the landlord is entitled to the *difference* between what the landlord would have received under the original lease and any new lease that he obtains.

Thus, if the breached lease leads to the landlord's higher profits, he may not collect damages. *United States Nat'l Bank of Oregon v. Homeland, Inc.* (Or. 1981).

D. Limits on the Lessor's Actions

A landlord may not recover unpaid rents from a tenant when the lease is *illegal*.

> *See Brown v. Southall Realty Co.* (D.C. App. 1968), where the defendant Brown failed to make certain rental payments and abandoned the apartment. The plaintiff lessor Southall sued for *possession and termination* of the lease. The defendant argued that the lease was illegal as against hygiene regulations and if a court granted the termination of the lease, it would make the lease valid *res judicata* in a future proceeding if the plaintiff sued to recover unpaid rent. Held: the lease, being in violation of housing regulations in place *before* the execution of the lease, is invalid. It may not be

terminated or used by the landlord as the grounds for collecting unpaid rent.

When a lease is invalid as against housing regulations, before evicting a tenant, a landlord may be required to either (i) make the necessary repairs and show a non-retaliatory reason to evict the defendant; or (ii) prove that he was going to take the housing off of the market.

> See also *Robinson v. Diamond Housing Corp.* (D.C. Cir. 1972), where the plaintiff sought to evict the defendant, who was not paying rent. The defendant invoked the *Brown v. Southall Realty Co.* defense: the lease was illegal because it was not in conformity with housing standards. The plaintiff then tried to evict the defendant, arguing that because there was no lease, the defendant should not be on the premises. The defendant invoked the thirty day notice defense. The plaintiff then gave the defendant sufficient notice and tried to evict her. The defendant invoked the *Edwards v. Habib* defense of retaliatory discharge. Held: perhaps because the court feared that if it allowed the plaintiff to evict the defendant, the plaintiff would simply rent it out to another tenant, it required the plaintiff to first show that he had either (i) made the necessary repairs and showed a non-retaliatory reason for evicting the defendant; or (ii) not made the repairs but was going to take the housing off of the market. In retaliatory discharge cases, then, in some states, the tenant can go on living in the housing unit indefinitely until the repairs are made.

VII.   ASSIGNMENTS AND SUBLEASES

A. Introduction

A transfer of property shifts the possession from one possessor to another. There are two kinds of transfers:

- A *sublease* grants possession of the land to a new tenant for *part of the duration of a lease period*, even if it is as little as one minute.
- An *assignment* grants the possession of land for the *entire period of the lease*. By default, an assignment grants *all of the property* for the lease period. A *partial assignment* may however, be granted for only *part of the property* for the lease period.

B. Determining Whether a Sublease or an Assignment has been Created

1. Common Law

Under the common law, if the first tenant has any reversion, even for one minute, a sublease has been created.

2. Modern Law

Under the modern law, the **intent** of the parties is *dispositive*.

> *See Jaber v. Miller* (Ark. 1951), where the landlord leased property to the defendant tenant Jaber, who subleased the property to a second party, who in turn subleased it to the plaintiff second sublessee Miller. The lease between the landlord and the defendant stipulated that *if there was a fire, the lease would be terminated.* There was a fire and the plaintiff sought cancellation of promissory notes he owed to the defendant under the agreement, arguing that his sublease was terminated because it was based on a sublease between the defendant and a second party, which terminated when the underlying lease between the landlord and the defendant was terminated. Held: the plaintiff's sublease was not cancelled because it is not carved out of a sublease between the defendant tenant and the second party; rather, it was carved out of an assignment. Under the modern law, we know that it is an assignment because the *intent of the parties is clear.* Thus, *the plaintiff has a continuing obligation to pay the defendant* because the assignment did not terminate, even though the lease between the landlord and the defendant expired. Judgment for the plaintiff reversed.

C. Privity

1. Overview

Suppose landlord 1 (L1) is in privity with this tenant (T1). L1 then sells the property to landlord 2 (L2). According to many sources, L2 and T1 are not in *privity of contract*. However, they are in privity of estate, since L2 owns the reversion.

To have privity of contract between T1 and L2, there must be **attornment**, where a party to a contract recognizes a new third party as a former party's valid successor to the contract. Here: it would be the tenant's recognition of the new owner and his agreement to pay rent to him.

2. Examples

a. *L1 and T1 are in privity of contract and privity of estate.*

b. *If T1 assigns his lease to T2, the resulting relationships are as follow:*

    -   L1-T1: privity of contract. L1 may look to T1 to continue to pay the rent. However, they are no longer in privity of estate.
    -   T1-T2: privity of contract. They would no longer be in privity of estate, since T1 no longer holds the estate.
    -   L1-T2: privity of estate. They are not in privity of contract, unless a lease is signed between them.
        o   Privity of estate carries with it all of the lease provisions between L1 and T1 that **run with the land**, including the payment of rent.
        o   As a result, L1 may look to T1 or T2 to pay rent.

c. *In the alternative, if T1 subleases the property to S2, the following relationships result:*

    -   L1-T1: privity of contract, privity of estate
    -   T1-S2: privity of contract, privity of estate
    -   L1-S2: no relationship

A sublessee is not liable to pay L1 for rent. However, since S2's lease is dependant on the L1-T1 lease, *S2 may not engage in activities prohibited by that lease.*

> Rationale: T1 cannot give away that which he does not have.
> Thus, if he owns only a limited possessory interest in the land, he may only give away that right to a sublessee.

Furthermore, when the L1-T1 lease is terminated, so too is the T1-S2 sublease, which is dependent on the former.

Thus, both T2's and S2's are obligated by at least some of the provisions in the L1-T1 lease, even though neither one is privy to it.

d. *Suppose L1 releases T1, and T2 agrees to assume T1's position with respect to L1 (this would be a case of* novation*). What are the relationships?*

    -   L1-T1: no privity
    -   T1-T2: no privity
    -   T2-L1: privity of contract, privity of estate

e. *Suppose L1 leases to T1 who transfers the property to T2 who transfers the property to T3. T3 defaults. Who may L1 go after?*
-   Can go after T1 (privity of contract);
-   T2 for the rent in the period in which L1 was in privity of estate with T2; or
-   T3 (privity of estate).

D. Landlord's Rights

1. Restrictions of Transfers by Landlords

Provisions in which a landlord restricts transfers of the property are generally disfavored by the courts. For the landlord to make a restriction, it must be explicit.

Courts will read such a restriction narrowly. For example, a *restriction on assignments does not restrict subleases*, unless the broad term "transfers" is used.

If there is such a provision, but a tenant nonetheless assigns or subleases the property, courts treat the landlord's acceptance of rent from the transferee as a waiver of the provision.

2. When the landlord makes a restriction, he may limit who his tenant transfers his lease to.

When there is a clause requiring the landlord's approval before the tenant subleases or assigns the property, the landlord's approval to the first transfer **does not mean that he waives his right to disapprove future transfers**.

According to the **Rule in Dumpor's Case**, however, once the landlord approves one transfer, he has *waived his right to disapprove others*.

However, when the lease **makes it clear** that the landlord has the right to approve multiple transfers, the landlord retains the right, even after the first approval. *Childs v. Warner Brothers Southern Theatres* (N.C. 1931).

3. The landlord **may act unreasonably** (for any reason or for no reason at all) in deciding who his tenant may transfer the property to.

> See *21 Merchants Row Corp. v. Merchants Row, Inc.* (Mass. 1992), where the defendant landlord Merchants Row, Inc. had a lease with the plaintiff lessee Merchants Row, Corp. that prevented the lessee

from assigning the lease without the defendant's consent. The plaintiff wanted to sell the business, but required the defendant's approval of the assignee. The plaintiff found an assignee that the defendant approved, but that assignee needed the plaintiff to approve an assignment to a bank that was going to finance the purchase. The defendant refused to grant it, since all the terms of the assignment would favor the bank. The plaintiff sued the defendant for breaching the contract in not allowing the assignment. Held: the court will not imply a reasonableness restriction on the defendant's right to reject potential assignees. Judgment for the defendant.

CHAPTER 2. THE ACQUISITION OF UNOWNED PROPERTY

I. THE ACQUISITION OF WILD ANIMALS AND UNOWNED PROPERTY

A. The Acquisition of Unowned Personal Property

1. *Ad Coelum* Doctrine

Under the *ad coelum* doctrine, for the purpose of immovable minerals, "to whomever the soil belongs, he also owns to the sky and to the depths." *See Edwards v. Sims* (Ky. 1929).

2. *Ratione Soli* Doctrine

Under the *ratione soli* doctrine, also known as "*ad coelum* minor," the owner of the soil *is the first occupant* and owner of whatever is found on the soil, including minerals and *ferae naturae*, regardless of who the finder is.

> *See Goddard v. Winchell* (Iowa 1892), where Winchell found a meteor on Goddard's property. Because the court applies the *ratione soli* doctrine, Goddard is able to replevy it.

This doctrine is not recognized by all states and even in those states that do recognize it, it is not always applied.

As we will explore later on, the more general rule allows finders to keep what they have found; the law grants finders better title than all the world except for the true owner, with some exceptions.

B. First Occupancy Theory

Under the first occupancy theory, the first occupant becomes the owner. The doctrine applies to the acquisition of *ferae naturae* (wild animals). However, the *ratione soli* doctrine continues to apply when an animal is captured and killed on someone's property.

When not captured and killed on another's property, *ferae naturae* belongs to the first occupant, regardless of whether the animal was originally on another's property.

The first occupant is the one who:

a. *Intends to possess and control an animal; and*

b. *Injures or traps it in a way that makes its escape either impossible or improbable, depending on the state's approach.*

-   Impossible (Strict Occupancy approach under *Pierson*)
    o   The animal's escape must be ***impossible***.
    o   *Mere pursuit* of an animal does not constitute ownership.
    o   Rather, one of the following must occur: (i) The animal must be trapped *and* escape must be impossible; or (ii) The animal must be mortally wounded *and* there is continued pursuit.

    See Pierson v. Post (N.Y. 1805), where the defendant was charged with unlawfully killing and capturing a fox that was under pursuit by the plaintiff. Held: mere pursuit of an animal does not constitute ownership. The animal would have had to be put into a situation where escape was impossible.

-   Improbable (Law of the Chase approach under *Liesner*).
    o   The animal's escape must be ***improbable***.
    o   If an animal is so badly wounded that escape will be made improbable, then the animal belongs to the party that wounded it. *See Leisner v. Wainie* (Wis. 1914).

II. ACQUISITION OF VOLATILE MINERALS (OIL AND GAS)

The general rule regarding minerals can be summarized by the *ad coelum* doctrine: the owner of a parcel of property has a right to the property as it extends "to the sky" and "to the depths." He becomes owner of all minerals beneath his land. *See Hammonds v. Central Kentucky Natural Gas Co.* (Ky.1934).

However, once volatile minerals are captured and stored, title to them is not lost, even if they migrate underneath another's land. The landowner may not exploit the stored mineral. *Lone Star Gas Co. v. Murchison* (Tex. Civ. App. 1962).

In summary, with respect to acquiring unowned property, courts apply:

- The *ad coelum* doctrine to the acquisition of fixed minerals and imbedded objects; and
- The *first occupant theory* to the acquisition of volatile minerals and *ferae naturae* (unless the *ferae naturae* is caught while on another's land).

III. ACQUISITION BY CONQUEST

When Europeans came to the Native Americans' land, the applicable rule was that the discoverer's government gained title to the land by conquest, despite the Native Americans' occupancy. Thus, courts held that one who was granted land by a Native American does not have good title, since the Native Americans did not have good title to transfer. *See Johnson v. McIntosh* (U.S. 1823).

CHAPTER 3. PERSONAL PROPERTY

I. BAILMENT

A. Overview

Bailment can be defined as a legally-recognized property relationship between a bailor, who delivers personalty to another to be held for a particular purpose, and a bailee, the party that receives the property.

The agreement between the bailor and the bailee can be written or oral, gratuitous or for consideration.

For there to be a bailment relationship, the following five elements must be met:

- The object of the bailment must be *personal property*;
- There must be actual or constructive *delivery* to the bailee[1];
- The bailee must expressly or impliedly *consent* to accepting the personal property;
- The bailee must have the *right of possession and actual possession*; and
- The bailee must agree to *return* the personal property back to the bailor, who maintains title.

B. Conditions under which the Bailee becomes Liable to the Bailor:

- If he fails to return the item, he becomes strictly liable.
- If he fails to exercise requisite care as bailee, the following standards of care apply:
    o The Modern Law Approach. An ordinary standard of care under the circumstances is *always required*. The bailee is thus liable for ordinary negligence.
    o The Three Approaches of the Common Law: (i) Gratuitous Bailment (solely beneficial to the bailor); (ii) Mutually Beneficial Bailment (mutually beneficial to the bailor and bailee; an ordinary standard of care is required); (iii) Bailment Solely Beneficial to the Bailee (when the

---

[1] An example of constructive delivery would be giving to another the keys to a car.

bailment only benefits the bailee, a high standard of care is required; the bailee is liable for even slight negligence).

Example: a store clerk finds in his store a mislaid wallet, which he intends to return to its rightful owner. If he loses the wallet, his standard of care will be:

Under the common law approach, he is subject to a slight duty of care (he is liable only for gross negligence).

Under the modern law approach, he has an ordinary standard of care under the circumstances; he is liable for ordinary negligence.

C. Burden of Providing Negligence

In trial, the burden of proving negligence in bailment cases falls on the plaintiff bailor. The plaintiff's *prima facie* case consists in proving: (i) he gave the personalty to the defendant in good condition; and (ii) the bailee did not return the personalty or return it back in a damaged condition.

When the problem was caused by abnormal causes, the burden is on the defendant to show that he was not at fault. If he is able to show he was not at fault, the burden shifts back to the plaintiff to show that the defendant was negligent in exposing the personalty to the risk of harm.

II. FINDINGS

A. Introduction to the Findings Law

The overarching goal of findings law is to get the item back to the original owner or to preserve the rights of the original owner.

At the same time, in order to promote honesty, finders are generally permitted to keep their findings. with the exceptions of the following circumstances, in which constructive possession is applied:

- Mislaid, imbedded property;
- Trespass;
- In other cases where the courts reserve the right to apply constructive possession.

B. Lost Items

The general rule of findings is that the finder obtains the right to possession against all of the world but the true owner.

See Bridges v. Hawkesworth (Q.B. 1851), where a man found a box of bank notes on the floor of a public section of a store and told the owner to hold it for the rightful owner. When the rightful owner never showed up, the finder asked for them back. The court held that the finder had the rightful title for the bank notes, since they were found in a public part of the store.

C. Mislaid Items

An item is mislaid when its owner intentionally places it in some place and then forgets about it.

An object will usually be considered to be mislaid when it is located on a table or a counter; it will be considered lost when found on the ground or some other area where it is unlikely to have been intentionally placed.

Possession of mislaid items is granted to the owner of the *locus in quo* (Lat., "place in which").

> *See McAvoy v. Medina* (Mass. 1866), where a wallet left on a table in a store was considered mislaid, not lost. The difference is between someone deliberately placing an object on a table and saying they will come to it later, but forgetting, and dropping it on the ground without any intention. When it is the former, the owner of the owner of the locus in quo, not the finder, obtains title.

D. Treasure Trove

Treasure trove is gold, silver, bullion, money, or coins found hidden under the ground when the true owner is unknown. For the purposes of possession, treasure trove can be treated as a ***lost item***, in that the true owner keeps title, and the finder is given possession until the true owner appears. This is perhaps to encourage finders to make their findings known.

However, not all courts recognize treasure trove. When a state does not recognize treasure trove, it will treat the question as an ordinary ***finding***, and will determine whether the object was *lost* or *mislaid*. *See Schley v. Couch* (Tex. 1955).

E. Imbedded Property

Imbedded property belongs to the owner of the locus in quo.

> *See South Staffordshire Water Co. v. Sharman* (Q.B. 1896), where the defendant, while working for the plaintiff, found rings imbedded

in the plaintiff's cesspool, which the defendant surrendered to the police and then kept when the true owner was not found. The plaintiff filed for detinue to recover the property or its value from the defendant. The court held that through *constructive possession*, the chattel should belong to the owner of the locus in quo rather than to the finder because it was found on private property.

See also Goddard v. Winchell (Iowa 1892), where possession of a meteor imbedded in the soil is granted to the owner of the locus in quo; ownership is not granted to the finder.

F. Constructive Possession

Constructive possession is control or dominion of property, as opposed to actual possession (physical occupancy).

Under the doctrine of constructive possession, control or dominion of property is granted to the owner of the owner of the locus in quo, in situations in which it would otherwise go to the finder (*e.g.*, in cases of treasure trove and findings generally).

There are no hard, fast rules as to when courts would apply this doctrine:

-   When an object lost in the public part of a store, a court probably *would not apply this doctrine*; the finder would obtain possession.
-   When an object is lost in a home or the private part of a store, a court would usually apply this doctrine; the owner of the locus in quo would get possession.

G. Abandoned items

First occupants of abandoned items acquire *full title*, even against the true owner. *See Eads v. Brazelton* (Ark. 1861). The occupant of an abandoned item must manifest the intent to exercise dominion and control and evidence that he is able to do so. In the example of *Eads v. Brazelton*, this would mean having a boat over the shipwreck that shows the intent to recover the cargo and the ability to do so.

H. Trespassing Finders

Trespassing finders relinquish control of found items to the owner of the locus in quo.

See *Favorite v. Miller* (Conn. 1978), where the owner of the locus in quo was able to keep the parts of a statue of King George that was found buried on his property, not only because it was imbedded in his soil, but also because it was taken by a trespasser.

I. Legislation Regulating Findings

Many states have adopted statutes regulating findings. Generally speaking, the statutes are different from the common law in that they:

- Tend to lump together lost and mislaid items;
- Require finders to turn in lost articles to police or face punishment; and
- Give a time limit after which items are returned to finders and another limit after which finders become owners.

III. PRIOR (UNAUTHORIZED) POSSESSION

Prior possession concerns when a prior wrongful possessor is able to replevy against a subsequent wrongful possessor. There are two approaches as to prior (unauthorized) possession:

A. Majority Approach

Under the majority approach, prior wrongful possessors are always allowed to recover the property, whether it is through trover (damages) or replevin of the property. *See Anderson v. Gouldberg* (Minn. 1892). *See also Clark v. Maloney* (Del. Super. Ct. 1840).

B. Minority Approach

Under the minority approach, prior (unauthorized) possessors are always allowed to seek to replevy the property. Prior possessors are also allowed to seek trover (damages) of the property as a general rule.

However, if the true owner is known, the prior possessor may not seek trover (damages); he may only replevy the property. This is because it is presumed that the true owner will ultimately try to recover the property through replevy.

Thus, if the subsequent unauthorized possessor is required to pay damages to the prior unauthorized possessor, the subsequent possessor will risk a double penalty if the true owner later seeks to replevy the property from him. He will have a double net loss, first having paid damages through trover to the prior possessor, and later giving up the property itself to the true owner through replevy.

To avoid this prejudicial treatment of the subsequent possessor, the courts in the minority approach only permit the prior possessor to seek replevin of the property from the subsequent possessor. It is presumed that if the true owner later tries to recover the property, he will replevy it against the prior possessor.

Thus, a double penalty will be imposed on neither the prior nor the subsequent possessor. Thus, under the minority approach, the prior possessor is only allowed to obtain trover *when the true owner is unknown*. Otherwise, the only possible recourse is replevin. *See Russell v. Hill* (N.C. 1899).

IV. ADVERSE POSSESSION

If a party takes possession of property of which he is not the lawful owner and maintains possession for a period prescribed by the statute of limitations in the local jurisdiction, he acquires rightful title if the lawful owner fails to oppose the wrongful possession.

The statute of limitations varies between jurisdictions, but can be as little as two years. With respect to real property, the possession should be a non-permissive use of the land with a claim of right by the adverse possessor.

The courts incrementally established that in order for the statute of limitations to run, the possession and use of the land must be:

- *Open* – the possession and use must not be hidden;
- *Continuous* – the defendant must have continuous possession throughout the running of the statute of limitations;
- *Exclusive* – the defendant must not share the possession with the true owner;
- *Adverse* – the wrongful possessor must claim and act as though he has title to the property; the claim must be adverse to the true owner's rights;
- *Notorious* – the use must suffice to put the true owner on notice that the adverse possessor is using the good and claiming title to it.
    - This element is virtually the same as the *open* element.
    - To meet the open and notorious elements, one must use the chattel in a way that it is normally used.

○ Examples: a store will openly display a wrongfully possessed ring; however, the owner of a ring may only wear it once per year if it is of great value.

A. Meeting the Statute of Limitations

1. Tacking

Many jurisdictions permit "tacking," which allows an adverse possessor to meet an adverse possession statute of limitations by adding together the periods in which previous possessors held the chattel.

The majority approach is to allow tacking; the minority approach is to require the adverse possessor claiming title to have possessed the property throughout the statute of limitations.

2. Tolling

Tolling, on the other hand, refers to the temporary stopping of the statute of limitations whenever one of the elements of adverse possession is not met.

3. The Discovery Rule

Sometimes, the statute of limitations begins to run not when the true owner is deprived of possession of his property, but rather, when he discovered or reasonably should have discovered the whereabouts of the chattel.

This rule, referred to as the "discovery rule," works to the benefit of the true owner.

Courts often apply this rule when meeting the adverse possession elements, to the disadvantage of the true owner, would be relatively easy for a possessor. *See O'Keeffe v. Snyder* (N.J. 1980).

B. Two Approaches to Good Faith

1. Majority Approach

Under the majority approach, merely possessing the property throughout the statute of limitations will confer title to the adverse possessor, when the possession is open, continuous, exclusive, adverse, and notorious.

2. Minority Approach

However, under the minority approach, in addition to meeting these elements, the possession must be with *good faith*. *See Riesinger's Jewelers, Inc. v. Roberson* (Okla.App.1978).

C. Elements of Adverse Possession

In order for an adverse possessor to win in a claim for a good, he must prove:

- His possession was open, continuous, exclusive, adverse, and continuous;
- He possessed the property throughout the statute of limitations;
  - o In the majority of jurisdictions, he may add on the periods in which the property was held by other possessors through tacking.
- He possessed in good faith (in minority jurisdictions);
  - o If tacking is permitted, the other possessors similarly must have possessed in good faith.
- The possession was within the *vicinity* (in the case of stolen chattels under *Riesinger's Jewelers v. Roberson*).

When all of these elements are met, the true owner loses his right to the property. Furthermore, under the "shelter principle," if one possessor can show that he became the owner under adverse possession (or some other ownership theory), then any subsequent possessor can claim that good title was also passed to him.

V. ACCESSION

A. Introduction

Accession is the acquisition of title to a thing through labor that transforms it into another thing. Under the general rule, an innocent trespasser does not gain title to a chattel through making improvements to it (the true owner can replevy the chattel), *unless* (i) the chattel is acquired in good faith; and (ii) *substantial* improvements are made to it. If both of these elements are met, title is transferred to the innocent trespasser and the true owner cannot replevy the chattel.

B. Elements

1. The object must be taken in ***good faith*** by the later improver.

Thus, if the object is taken by a thief, no amount of improvement will cause title to transfer (this is the American approach, which follows the civil law, not the common law approach).

This does not require that *all* prior possessors have good faith.

> Example: if a good faith possessor purchases a chattel from a thief, and later makes substantial improvements to it, he may acquire title. *See Capitol Chevrolet Co. v. Earhart* (Tenn. Ct. App. 1981).

The chattel must be transformed into a new chattel of **substantially greater value** from the time it comes into the later improver's hands. The improvements made to the chattel must not be easily separable from it. Normally, the improvements must be so substantial that the value of the chattel increases by a factor of fifteen or more (depending on what the item is).

> Example: a later improver will acquire title to timber that was originally valued at $25, when, with good faith, he transformed it into hoops valued at $700. *Wetherbee v. Green* (Mich. 1871).

Note that this element does not require that a fifteen-factor improvement of the property is measured from the time that the property leaves the true owner's hands to the time that the improvements are made; rather, it is measured from the time that the property is delivered to the later improver to the time that the improvements are made.

> Example: a thief steals a car valued at $15,000 and strips it down to a value of $1,000. A good faith purchaser purchases the car for $1,000 and makes improvements that bring the value of the car back up to $15,000.
>
> Although the improvements did not increase the value of the car from its *original* value, the later improver will obtain title, since substantial improvements were made from the time the car was delivered to him.

C. The True Owner's Remedies

If either of the elements of accession are not met—the later improver fails to act in good faith or he fails to make *substantial* improvements to the chattel—the true owner may **replevy** the chattel.

When the later improver lacks good faith, the true owner may replevy the chattel, no matter much labor and value the improver put into the good.

However, if he acts in good faith but fails to make *substantial* improvements, he may keep the improvements if they are separable from the original object. If they are not, the true owner acquires them when he replevies the chattel.

If a later improver acts in good faith *and* makes substantial improvements, although the true owner may not replevy the chattel, he may obtain *damages* equal to the value of the chattel at the time that it was delivered to the later improver (*e.g.*, $25 in the case of *Wetherbee*).

VI. *BONA FIDE* PURCHASE

A. Overview

We have already examined two theories of ownership in which an owner may be deprived of property without his consent—adverse possession and accession.

We now turn our attention to a third theory where an owner may similarly be deprived of property without his consent—*bona fide* purchase.

B. Elements of *Bona Fide* Purchase:
- Purchases in good faith;
- Without notice of fraud;
  - o Notice of fraud is knowledge that someone else owns a chattel.
  - o This element requires that the plaintiff ask questions that would give notice of fraud. *Porter v. Wertz* (N.Y. App. Div. 1979).
- For value.
  - o The property may not be given as a gift or at a price that is so substantially below the market value that it is considered to be a gift.
  - o It must be purchased at the market value or the appropriate value under the circumstances.

C. *Caveat Emptor*

1. General Principle

The general principle of *bona fide* purchase is *caveat emptor* ("buyer beware"). The *bona fide* purchaser does not acquire title to a good when the seller did not have title to transfer. A seller may not transfer better title than he has.

2. Exceptions

a. Overview

The following exceptions to the *caveat emptor* ruling principle are recognized by the common law and statutes:

- Under **equitable estoppel**, which is governed by the common law, there are two exceptions to *caveat emptor*:
  o Voidable title; and
  o Apparent authority.
- Under **statutory estoppel**, which applies to the sale of goods and is governed by the UCC,[2] there are two exceptions to *caveat emptor*:
  o Voidable title; and
  o Entrustment.

All of these exceptions permit the *bona fide* purchaser to keep title because of some action of the original owner that prohibits him from later replevying the chattel.

b. Common Law Voidable Title

i. General Rule

When the original owner has the intent to transfer title, voidable title passes, even if title is obtained through fraud (*e.g.*, where the original owner intended to transfer title to one purchaser, but was defrauded into transferring title to another purchaser). *Phelps v. McQuade* (N.Y. 1917).

This voidable title ripens into full title when it is transferred to a *bona fide* purchaser *for value*.

---

[2] The Uniform Commercial Code (UCC), which is enacted with some variations in all fifty states, governs the statutory estoppel exceptions to the principle of *caveat emptor*.

Rationale: when the original owner had some intent to transfer title, the result can be to some extent imputed to his neglect or other conduct.

N.B.: title is not passed when a party fraudulently represents himself to be an agent of another.

However, when the original owner had no intention of transferring title, *no title* passes. The sale must be face to face; voidable title does not pass when it is done through letter or by agent.

ii. Theft

Since there is no intent to transfer title when a chattel is stolen, thieves do not obtain voidable title or any other transferable title. *See Lieber v. Mohawk Arms* (N.Y. 1970).

Even when the thief makes improvements to the stolen good, he obtains neither full nor voidable title. *See National Retailers Mut. Ins. Co. v. Gambino* (N.J. Sup. Ct. App. Div. 1948).

Although voidable title becomes full title when it is transferred to a *bona fide* purchaser *for value*, the title of a thief is void and remains void, even if transferred to a *bona fide* purchaser.

iii. Bailees

Since bailors have no intent to transfer title, bailees do not obtain voidable title and therefore have no title to pass.[3] *Baehr v. Clark* (Iowa 1891). Because the title of a bailee is void, it remains void, even if transferred to a *bona fide* purchaser.

c. *Common Law Apparent Authority*

Under this second exception, even if an original owner has no intent to sell a good, voidable title passes if the original owner, through some level of conduct, clothes the possessor with the apparent authority to sell. Under this exception, the possessor's acts are imputed to the original owner.

> *See O'Connor v. Clark* (Pa. 1895), where the original owner of a wagon painted the name of his new employee on the wagon. When the employee transferred the wagon to a third party, the court granted

---

[3] However, under the entrustment exception of the UCC, discussed *infra.*, a merchant may pass voidable title of bailed chattel entrusted to him when he sells them to a buyer in the ordinary course of business.

title to the defendant *bona fide* purchaser through the employee's apparent authority to transfer title. The original owner was estopped from denying that his employee was the owner.

d. Voidable Title under the UCC

"A purchaser of goods acquires all title that the purchaser's transferor had or had power to transfer." UCC § 2-403(1).

> Example: if a thief steals a chattel from an original owner and later sells it, the later purchaser does not receive title, since the thief had no title to transfer.

However, a seller sometimes has power to transfer more title than he actually had: holders of voidable title may transfer good title to *good faith purchasers* for *value*. UCC § 2-403(1).

Voidable title is passed when the original owner has the intention to pass title (generally, the original owner owner somehow acts negligently).

As long as goods are delivered under a transaction, voidable title passes, even if:

- The purchaser *deceives the seller* as to his identity;
- The goods are procured through a *bounced check*;
- The transaction was by a "*cash sale*" (*e.g.*, the buyer promises to later deliver cash for a chattel that the seller immediately delivers); or
- The original owner is induced to sell to a wrongful possessor through "*fraud punishable as larcenous* under the criminal law" (*e.g.*, stealing and using another's credit card, using counterfeit money, etc.). UCC § 2-403(1).

Under the UCC, voidable title may pass by letter or face to face.

e. Entrustment under the UCC

The above-mentioned voidable title and apparent authority exceptions discuss when voidable title may pass to a *bona fide* purchaser.

The entrustment exception under the UCC, in contrast, deals with when voidable title may pass to a buyer in ordinary course of business (BOC).

A BOC may obtain good title from a merchant who sells bailed chattel entrusted to him for repair, improvement, etc., when the merchant deals in goods of that kind. UCC § 2-403(2).

A BOC must:

- Purchase with good faith;
- Without notice of fraud;
- From a business establishment in the ordinary course of business.

  N.B.: a purchase would *not be in the ordinary course of business* if a merchant over his lunch hour takes his client to his home to sell him a chattel.

Note that, unlike the voidable title exceptions to *bona fide* purchase, it is not necessary to show that the purchase was "for value"; since the chattel is being purchased from a business, it is assumed that the BOC paid market value.

VII.　GIFTS

A gift, or donative transfer, is a present, voluntary transfer of title without consideration.

A. Classes

1. *Inter Vivos* Gifts

Inter vivos gifts are given while donor is living. They are not revocable.

2. *Mortis Causa* Gifts

Mortis causa gifts are given in anticipation of the donor's death. They can be revoked if:

- The donee dies before the donor;
- The donor does not die from the anticipated illness and does not decide to give the gift *inter vivos*;
- The donor revokes the gift before he dies but while he is still ill.

B. Elements

1. Donative Intent

The donor must *intend* to *presently transfer* title to the donee. If the transfer will take place in the future, it is not a gift, but rather, a promise that is unenforceable if it lacks consideration.

2. Delivery

The donor must deliver the chattel. The delivery may take on any of the following forms:

- *Actual delivery*: the donee physically takes possession of the chattel.
- *Constructive delivery*: where the donor that which is necessary for possessing the chattel (*e.g.*, the keys to a car).
- *Delivery by written instrument*: the instrument must show the intent to transfer, be signed by the donor, describe the subject matter of the gift, and be delivered;
- *Symbolic delivery*: the donor delivers some object that symbolizes the gift (*e.g.*, a cow could symbolize one's entire herd).

3. Acceptance

The donee must accept the chattel. Acceptance is often presumed if a gift is unconditional and beneficial.

Courts require the best possible delivery under the circumstances. Generally, a signed, executed deed is sufficient. Some courts have held that such a document comprised delivery *even when it was not actually delivered.*

> *See In re Cohn* (N.Y. 1919), where the court held that a signed, executed agreement granting the decedent's wife a donative transfer of stocks was held valid, even though it was never actually delivered. *N.B.*: this case holding is exceptional; courts generally require actual delivery, unless precluded by the circumstances.

Symbolic delivery in the form of a written instrument has also been held to be sufficient. Other courts have held that clear and unequivocal intent on its own is sufficient when delivery is impossible.

> In *Scherer v. Hyland* (N.J. 1977), Wagner committed suicide, leaving a check and letter for Scherer to recover. Since the letter and the fact that only Wagner had access to that space gave adequate evidence that Wagner intended to give check as gift, the court "imported" delivery, even though there was no actual delivery.

CHAPTER 4. CONVEYANCES AND ACQUIRING TITLE

I. FINANCING ARRANGEMENTS

A. Introduction

There are two ways in which a vendee may purchase land without paying at once: through mortgages and through installment land contracts.

B. Mortgages

A mortgage is essentially a security for a debt. The mortgagee, or lender, receives the mortgage, which usually looks like a deed. If the mortgagor, or borrower, defaults on a payment, the mortgage allows the mortgagee to obtain possession of the property, usually after a hearing with proof of default in payments by the mortgagor.

Mortgages have *defeasance clauses* that recognize that, once the debt has been paid, the mortgage is no longer of any effect.

Documents involved in a deed:

- The *deed of trust*, which conveys title of the property; and
- The *note*, which makes mortgagors personally liable in case a property sale or foreclosure does not raise all of the funds.

1. Default and Title

At common law, the mortgage operates as a conveyance of title to the mortgagee, who holds the mortgage. However, *the title only becomes active* if the mortgagor defaults on his payments. Even a single default payment at common law allowed the mortgagee to keep all past payments, possess the land, and sell it to recover the money due.

In many other states, a mortgage was not considered to grant title to the mortgagee. Rather, it is viewed as a *mere lien*.

To offset the harsh effects of the common law, the **equitable right of redemption** developed to allow the mortgagor to redeem his property (this doctrine is recognized in all states). Generally, the mortgagor may redeem the property by paying the amount due, plus interest. If he has defaulted on a mortgage note requiring the full balance in the event of a default, then he must *pay the entire balance to redeem* the property.

In about half the states, the mortgagor's right of redemption continues even **after the foreclosure** sale. The redemption period is set by statute and usually lasts from six to twelve months. The mortgagor may usually redeem the property by paying the foreclosure sale price.

Today, most states view the mortgage not as **title** to the property, but as a mere **lien**.

There are two approaches to foreclosure that correspond to the views states have adopted with respect to the mortgage and the title-bearer of the mortgaged property:

- Foreclosure by Sale
  - o This is the approach in **lien theory states**, which treat the mortgage as a lien on the land to repay a loan.
  - o After the redemption period expires, the property is sold and the mortgagee returns to the mortgagor monies raised beyond the original debt.
  - o Today, most states view the mortgage as a lien. Foreclosure by sale is therefore the *majority approach*.
- Strict Foreclosure
  - o This is the approach in **title theory states**, which treat the mortgage as an instantaneous, actual transfer of title.
  - o Once an action is brought and the statutory period passes, the title actually changes hands and is transferred to the mortgagee (lender), who becomes the owner of the property.
  - o Strict foreclosure follows the common law, which today is the minority approach.

C. Installment Land Contracts

In installment land contracts, also known as "land contracts" or "conditional land contracts," the purchaser is granted possession, but the vendor retains title, in contrast to the mortgage, where in most states today, title passes to the mortgagor.

The purchaser pays the vendor in periodic installments and, when he completes the requisite payments, he receives title. Installment land contracts are typically used when a buyer is unable to acquire a mortgage to purchase the land.

Traditionally, courts enforce *forfeitures* (strict foreclosures) in installment land contracts in a summary manner. Thus, if purchaser defaults, the vendor may keep the land, as in a "summary," or "strict" foreclosure (forfeiture).

Exception: when the forfeiture is unequivocally unjust.

Some states, however, by statute, allow the purchaser to pay off the accelerated full balance of the contract and keep the land (this parallels the equitable right of redemption for mortgages).

Some states have also passed statutes that impose grace periods, allowing the purchasers to redeem the land.

Courts consider a series of factors in determining whether to allow forfeiture in installment land contracts, including whether the purchaser has made most of the payments, whether he has made substantial improvements to the property, and whether the forfeiture provision allows the creditor to keep all monies paid as well as the defaulted land. *See Skendzel v. Marshall* (Ind. 1973).

II. MERCHANTABLE TITLE

A. Introduction

Merchantable title is title that is not subject to such reasonable doubt that it would create a just apprehension of its validity in the mind of a reasonable prudent person.

Title that would be subject to a substantial risk of litigation is not considered merchantable. However, merchantable title is not necessarily good title; it may have *slight defects* do not invalidate the title (*e.g.*, a missing signature in one of the preceding title holders' deeds; an unaccounted for period in the history of land ownership; etc).

B. The Implied Warranty of Merchantable Title

In every land sale contract, an implied warranty of merchantable title guarantees that the seller will present and pass merchantable title to the purchaser *at the closing* ("law day"), unless the parties have contracted otherwise.

If the seller does not have merchantable title at the time that the land sale contract is formed, he may acquire it during the executory period (the period between the formation of the contract and the closing).

If there are outstanding liens that would breach the warranty of merchantable title, the seller may rely on a portion of the sale proceeds in escrow to remove the liens, as long as the purchaser is assured that the escrow funds will not be released until after the removal of the liens.

If the seller fails to obtain merchantable title before law day, the purchaser may rescind the contract and seek restitution. Until then, a buyer may not sue for rescission and restitution.

> *See Luette v. Bank of Italy Nat. Trust and Savings Association* (9th Cir. 1930). *Exception*: when property is so badly encumbered that the plaintiff may reasonably assume that the defendant will not have the merchantable title at the time that the last payment is due, the defendant may be required to offer merchantable title before law day.

The parties may, however, limit the implied warranty of merchantable title. Very specific language is required. The language, "buyer agrees to purchase *all of the seller's interest in his premises,*" or, "*all of the seller's interest, whether or not he has full title,*" is sufficient in overcoming the implied warranty of merchantable title.

> *N.B.*: under this contract, if the buyer later discovers that the seller did not have merchantable title, he *may not rescind* the contract before or after law day.

However, if the contract states that the buyer "agrees to accept the land located at X location" or "all of the seller's premises," the implied warranty is not overcome. If the seller fails to present merchantable title at the closing, the buyer may rescind the contract. If the contract states that the buyer "agrees to accept all of the seller's premises by *quitclaim deed,*" the implied warranty is not overcome, and the buyer has the right to *rescind the contract* if he finds that the seller did not have merchantable title. *See Wallach v. Riverside Bank* (N.Y. 1912).

C. Two Remedies for Breach of the Implied Warranty of Merchantable Title

1. Specific Performance

A court may require the seller to acquire merchantable title before law day, when doing so is practical. For example, if there is a lien on the property, a court may require the seller to clear it with the money received from the sale.

2. Rescission and Restitution

This is awarded when (i) specific performance (SP) is neither practical nor possible; or (ii) the contract does not provide for SP. *See Bartos v. Czerwinski* (Mich. 1948).

III. EQUITABLE CONVERSION AND RISK OF LOSS

A. The Doctrine of Equitable Conversion

There are three steps in the process of transferring title to property: (i) the *land sale contract*; (ii) the delivery of *merchantable (marketable) title*; and (iii) the *closing*. There is always a question as to who "owns" the land in the executory period between the formation of the contract and the closing and who bears the risk of loss.

Under the **doctrine of equitable conversion**, the purchaser is the owner of the property and bears the risk of loss from the moment the contract is executed.

This doctrine is based on the equity rationale that "what ought to be done is considered done." Since a contract ought to be followed, the buyer is considered to be the title-holder, even when he does not yet have the deed or possession of the land.

However, the doctrine of equitable conversion does not apply in the following circumstances:

- Contractual provisions that state otherwise (e.g., "title shall remain with the seller");
- Vendor's negligence, where the seller damages the property during the executory period and the buyer only finds out when he takes the property;
- Misrepresentation or fraud by a party;
- The inexistence of a binding contract;
- The inexistence of marketable title; or
- Changed circumstances that frustrate the purchaser's purpose. *See Clay v. Landreth* (Va. 1948).

B. The Three Approaches to the Effect of the Risk of Loss

1. Majority Approach

Under the majority approach, title is transferred to the buyer at the execution of the contract and the buyer bears the risks of loss during the executory period (in the absence of the above-described exceptions). *See Bleckley v. Langston.*

2. Minority Approach

Under the minority approach, the seller keeps title upon execution of the contract and retains the risk of loss during the executory period; he may collect damages if, after loss, the plaintiff decides not to go forward with the closing. This is the approach adopted in Massachusetts.

3. Uniform Vendor and Purchaser Risk Act

If the Uniform Vendor and Purchaser Risk Act has been adopted, the doctrine of equitable conversion will not be applied when unanticipated damages occur.

Instead, the contract will be rescinded and any money paid by the purchaser will be restituted to him. The vendor will not be entitled to damages. However, the purchaser assumes the risk of loss when either legal title or possession is transferred to him.

IV. THE MODERN DEED

A. Introduction

1. A deed has the following elements:
   - It must be written;
   - It must contain:
     o The names of the parties;
     o A granting clause;
     o A legal description of the property (the subject matter conveyed); and
     o A signature (for the Statute of Frauds).
   - It must be delivered.
     o Delivery refers to the mental state of the grantor, not to the physical custody of the deed.
     o Thus, even if the deed is not physically delivered to the purchaser, the deed is deemed to be delivered if the grantor evidences an intent to presently transfer title.

○ An undelivered deed is completely void and can pass no interest in the land, even if it is later recorded. *Stone v. French* (Kan. 1887).

2. Other parts of the deed

Some deeds also tend to include, but do not require: (i) the *stated consideration*; (ii) a *habendum clause* limiting the rights being conveyed (*e.g.*, a right to possess but not to disposed of the property); and (iii) a *redendum clause* reserving any interest in the property to the seller (*e.g.*, easements).

In the old common law, a deed required a seal to be valid. In most states today, this requirement has been abolished.

B. Construing Deeds

Inconsistent parts within a deed must be reconciled by the courts. When all else is equal, a **granting clause** trumps an **inconsistent habendum clause**. *See First Nat'l Bank of Oregon v. Townsend* (Or. 1976).

Although the granting clause trumps the *habendum* clause, the *intent of the parties* may rebut the granting clause. *See Grayson v. Holloway* (Tenn. 1958).

V. THE RECORDING SYSTEM

A. Introduction

The purpose of recording a deed is to protect present owners from subsequent *bona fide* purchasers. If a *bona fide* purchaser purchases property in good faith for value without notice from a seller who is not the true owner of the property being sold, he may acquire title to the land **if the true owner failed to record his deed**.

If, however, the true owner recorded the deed, the *bona fide* purchaser would be charged with constructive notice and no title would pass.

Although recording a deed is not an essential element to the validity of the deed, recording the deed is an important step towards protecting one's property interest.

B. Four Approaches to Recordings

1. The Common Law Approach

Under the common law, the party with the **earlier deed** obtains title and possession to the property conveyed.

2. The Three Statutory Approaches

a. Notice Approach

A subsequent grantee wins if he is a *bona fide* purchaser who purchases in **good faith** for **value without notice**, regardless of when he actually records.

> See Earle v. Fiske (Mass. 1870), where decedent Nancy Fiske conveys land to Benjamin and Elizabeth Fiske as a life estate, with the remainder to Mary Fiske, but does not record the transaction. Upon Nancy's death, her only heir Benjamin sold the land to the plaintiff Earle, who **purchased the property in good faith without notice for value**. The plaintiff sued for a writ of entry. Held: since Massachusetts is a notice state, the **only requirement** for passing title is that **the plaintiff have no** actual or constructive **notice** of the other property interest and that the plaintiff pay value. These elements are met, since the plaintiff was on neither actual nor constructive notice that Benjamin did not have fee title to transfer. Title is vested in the plaintiff.

b. Race/Notice Approach

A subsequent grantee wins only if he (i) is a **bona fide purchaser**; and (ii) **records first**. A *bona fide* purchaser thus will not win against another purchaser who recorded first. *See Simmons v. Stum* (Ill. 1882) .

c. Pure Race

The grantee who **records first** wins title.

C. Two Systems for Searching for Records on One's Property:
-   The **grantor/grantee index**, which is a list of all previous owners of a tract; and
-   The **tract index,** which is a list of every tract and its particular owner and all recorded instruments affecting it. This index greatly facilitates the ability of prospective purchases to find if there is good title and to discover restrictions on the property.

D. Records of Easements

Parties are on ***constructive notice*** of easements on land that they are purchasing when those easements are ***in the original deeds of record***. ***Contractors*** do not have this same duty to examine those records. *See Mountain States Telephone and Telegraph Co. v. Kelton* (Ariz. 1955).

CHAPTER 5. THE INTEGRITY OF THE LAND

I. TRESPASS AND NUISANCE; SUPPORT OF LAND

A. Trespass and Nuisance

A nuisance is a condition or activity on another's land that unreasonably affects the other's right to enjoy and use his land. The standard is one of a *person of ordinary sensibility*.

Factors considered in determining whether a condition is a nuisance include whether:

- The condition begins or occurs after the plaintiff has been occupying the land;
- The condition has little value to the one causing it;
- The activity has little social value; and
- The activity lowers the value of the owner's property.

B. Burdens of Proof

If the owner of the land meets his burden of proving (i) **causation**; and (ii) **damages**, an injunction will be granted.

However, the defendant may raise a defense and avoid an injunction by showing that either: (i) the damage is unavoidable; or (ii) the cost of avoiding the damage is so high that it would deprive the defendant of the use of the land. *See Renken v. Harvey Aluminum* (D. Or. 1963).

If either of these elements are met by the defendant, a court will **balance the equities** by looking to each side's interests in order to determine whether to award damages or an injunction.

> Example: if granting an injunction against the activities of a major factory would cause a substantial loss of profits and the loss of thousands of jobs, a court may instead grant money damages to the plaintiff, especially when it appears that such a remedy would make the plaintiff whole.

Furthermore, courts will not grant injunctions when doing so would entangle the judiciary in national policy areas generally reserved for legislatures. *See Boomer v. Atlantic Cement Co.* (N.Y. 1970).

C. Public and Private Nuisances

1. Private Nuisance

A nuisance is private when the party whose property interest is being disturbed is one individual or a few individuals, as opposed to an entire neighborhood or community.

The owner of the land being disturbed may recover for any nuisances against the defendant when he can prove causation and damages. He will obtain at least money damages, and possibly an injunction.

However, when the nuisance existed when the owner purchased the land (*"coming to the nuisance"*), the owner will not recover, unless the nuisance has become greater in degree since the land purchase.

2. Public Nuisance

A nuisance is public when the parties whose property interest is being disturbed are large groups of individuals or an entire community.

The plaintiffs may recover from the defendant for any nuisances when they can prove causation and damages, *including when they "come to the nuisance." See Spur Industries, Inc. v. Del E. Webb Development Co.* (Ariz. 1972).

II. ZONING

A. Introduction

Zoning occurs when a legislature limits the permitted uses of the land. Example: a ban on easily ignitable building materials in a part of town that is susceptible to fires. Among the purposes of zoning are aesthetic values, health, safety, and welfare.

B. Constitutionality

All zoning laws, to be valid, must be deemed constitutional. The following two-part test is applied:

-   The law must have a ***proper purpose*** (*i.e.*, a purpose within the police power of the state (morality, health, safety, welfare);
    o   A proper purpose may be aesthetic value.

- o However, the zoning standard is unconstitutional when arbitrarily applied. *Nectow v. City of Cambridge* (U.S. 1928).
- The law must reasonably promote that purpose.

When these elements are met, the law is deemed *constitutional, even if it causes a decrease in the value* of the property affected. *See Village of Euclid v. Ambler Realty Co.* (U.S. 1926).

III. TAKINGS

A. Introduction

A taking is an appropriation of private property by the state for the common good. Property is considered to be "taken" when it is *actually taken* (*i.e., physically invaded* and *appropriated*) or so *heavily regulated* that the owner has been deprived of all economic use.

B. Actual Takings

Under the Fifth Amendment Takings Clause, private property shall not "be taken for public use, without just compensation." There are thus two requirements for valid public takings:

- "Just compensation" must be paid.
  - o Just compensation must be a "full and perfect equivalent" of the value of the property.
- They must be done for a legitimate "public use."
  - o Today, however, the inquiry no longer looks into whether a taking is based on a legitimate public use; rather, the courts search for *any legitimate public purpose*, which may include: (i) Land redistribution from a small oligarchy to the general public; and (ii) The development of a blighted sector.
  - o The purpose need not benefit all of the public; it is sufficient if only some benefit.
  - o Furthermore, a taking need not transfer ownership to the government; it may transfer ownership **to private interests**. *See Hawaii Housing Authority v. Midkiff* (U.S. 1984). *See also Kelo v. City of New London* (U.S. 2005) (Stevens, J.).

o   However, where the government's transfer of interests between private interests is done *for the sole purpose of transferring ownership*, the taking is *unconstitutional*, even if just compensation is paid.

C. Regulatory Takings

As mentioned above, property is considered to be "taken" not only when it is *actually appropriated*, but also when it is so *heavily regulated* that the owner has been deprived of all economic use of his land. When property is "taken" through burdensome regulation, just compensation must be paid.

There are two kinds of regulatory takings that require just compensation:

- Physical Invasions
  See, e.g., Loretto v. Teleprompter Manhattan CATV Corp. (U.S. 1982), where the installations of cables in apartment buildings constituted a taking, even though only an insignificant space in the apartments was occupied. The taking was imputed to the government, since a local law required certain property owners to permit the installations.

- Regulations Denying All Economically Beneficial Use of the Land
  See Lucas v. South Carolina Coastal Council (U.S. 1992), where the Beachfront Management Act barred the plaintiff from any economically profitable use of land that he purchased for $975,000. Held (Scalia, J.): the act's effect on the plaintiff's ability to economically benefit from his land was a key factor for determining whether just compensation was required.

APPENDICES

THEMATIC INDEX

TABLE OF CASES

GLOSSARY

A

Absolute majority A majority consisting of at least half of the votes cast plus one or, stated in another form, more than half of the votes. An absolute majority requires more votes in favor than abstentions and votes against combined. *Compare* SIMPLE MAJORITY and QUALIFIED MAJORITY.

Accord Agreement that a debt obligation be settled for less than the creditor is entitled. *Compare* SATISFACTION.

Accord and satisfaction *See* ACCORD *and* SATISFACTION (separately).

Ad coelum **doctrine** Under this doctrine, for the purpose of immovable minerals, "to whomever the soil belongs, he also owns to the sky and to the depths." It refers to the right of the owner of property to the space that extends vertically upward and downward from his property.

Administrative law Set of legal regulations that govern the activities of governmental administrative agencies. Administrative law deals with the decision-making of administrative units of government, such as tribunals or commissions. In the US, administrative law focuses on the actions of executive agencies and independent agencies.

Arson The malicious, willful, and unlawful burning of a structure which, at common law, had to be the dwelling place of another.

Assignment A transfer of property that grants the possession of land for the *entire period of a lease*. By default, an assignment grants *all of the property* for the lease period. A *partial assignment* may however, be granted for only *part of the property* during the lease period. *Compare* SUBLEASE.

B

Bailment A legally recognized property relationship between a bailor, who gives personalty to another to be held for a particular purpose, and a bailee, party that receives the property.

Bank guarantee Unconditional undertaking given by a bank or other lending institution on behalf of a client buyer or debtor to pay a third party the amount of the guarantee on written demand in the event the client fails to settle debt or otherwise deliver payment. *Compare* LETTER OF CREDIT.

Bill of attainder An uconstitutional legislative action that singles out an individual or group for punishment without the benefit of a trial.

Burglary At common law, the specific intent crime that consisted of the breaking and entering of the dwelling of another at night with the intent to commit a felony therein.

C

Causation in fact Actual causation that links an act with a result through implementing the "but-for" test (*i.e.*, "but for A, B would not have occurred"). *Compare* PROXIMATE CAUSE.

Circumstantial evidence Secondary facts and other evidence that lead to primary fact inferences.

Chattel An item of personal, as opposed to real property; any moveable object.

Claim preclusion *See* RES JUDICATA.

Closing (real property) The final meeting between the seller and the purchaser in a land sale contract, whereby the executory period is concluded and the payment and property are exchanged.

Closing of escrow *See* CLOSING.

Collateral estoppel Under the doctrine of collateral estoppel, a factual issue *may not be litigated* in any lawsuit if it was litigated and decided in a previous proceeding. *Also known as* ISSUE PRECLUSION.

Consent decree Final, binding judicial decree or judgment memorializing a voluntary agreement between parties to a lawsuit in return for withdrawal of a criminal charge or an end to a civil litigation. In a typical consent decree, the defendant has already ceased or agrees to cease the conduct alleged by the plaintiff to be illegal and consents to a court injunction barring the conduct in the future. Sometimes the defendant does not expressly admit fault, illegality or damages. Consent decrees are used most commonly in criminal and family law. They are frequently used by the US Securities and Exchange Commission. *Also known as* CONSENT ORDER or STIPULATED JUDGMENT or AGREED JUDGMENT.

Consequential damages Legal damages for a foreseeable loss that are an indirect consequence of a breach of contract or other wrongful act. For example, if a courier failed to deliver a parcel, the dispatcher's lost revenues as a result of the non-delivery are the consequential damages. *Also known as* SPECIAL DAMAGES or INDIRECT DAMAGES. *Compare* DIRECT DAMAGES *and* INCIDENTAL DAMAGES.

Consideration The concept of legal value in connection with contracts. It can be anything of value, including money, services, or any abstinence from a future action that is promised to another when making a contract. With some exceptions, in order for a promise to be enforceable, it must be supported by consideration.

Consignee In a contract of carriage, the party receiving a shipment to be delivered by land, sea or air, to be received by a CONSIGNEE. *Also known as* Recipient. In a contract for sale, the CONSIGNEE receives goods from a CONSIGNOR that it tries to sell on the CONSIGNOR'S behalf.

Consignor In a contract of carriage, the party sending a shipment to be delivered by land, sea or air, to be received by a CONSIGNEE. *Also known as* Sender. In a contract of sale, the CONSIGNOR sends goods to a CONSIGNEE to sell on the CONSIGNOR'S behalf.

Constructive notice Legal notice derived from the circumstances.

Construction The act of interpreting the sense or intention of a constitution, statute, contract, or some other text; the process of construing the meaning of a writing.

Constructive possession doctrine Doctrine by which control or dominion of property is granted to the owner of the *locus in quo*, in situations in which it would otherwise go to the finder (*e.g.*, in cases of treasure trove and findings generally). The doctrine is applied, for example, when an object is found in a private place of a store. The owner of the *locus in quo*, rather than the finder, obtains possession.

Conversion A tortious act of willful interference with the property of another without lawful justification, in a way that *deprives the owner of the use of his property*. Examples of conversion include illegal takings, the assumption of ownership, and the destruction of the property of another.

Counterclaim An independent cause of action made by the defendant against the plaintiff in order to defeat the plaintiff's claim.

Criminal negligence Extremely negligent conduct that creates a risk of death or serious bodily injury beyond that of mere civil negligence.

Cross-claim A claim under FRCP 13(g) by one party against a co-party arising out of the transaction or occurrence that is the subject matter either of the original action or of a counterclaim therein or relating to any property that is the subject matter of the original action.

Cumulative voting Helps strengthen the ability of minority shareholders to elect a director, since it allows shareholders to cast all of their votes for a single nominee when the company has multiple openings on its board. If cumulative voting were banned, a winner-take-all election could result in no minority shareholder having enough shares to appoint a member. For example, a minority shareholder could cumulate his 20% share in a company to vote his 20% three times in one election for a director, thereby gaining a 60% majority, rather than watering down his vote to 20% in three separate election where he would be unlikely to win any one of them.

D

Dead Man's Act A statute that disqualifies a party from testifying *against the estate* of the deceased because of the party's incentive to lie based on: (i) his interest in the case; and (ii) the unavailability of the deceased to contradict him.

Defamation False accusation of an offense or a malicious misrepresentation of someone's words or actions that damages or destroys the good fame or reputation of a person, business or other entity. *See* LIBEL and SLANDER.

Detinue An action at common law to recover PERSONALTY or its value when it is unlawfully held by another.

Devise To make a gift of real property by will. Property that can be given in such a gift is referred to as "devisable."

Direct damages Legal damages for a loss that are directly, immediately, naturally, and foreseeably related to a breach of contract or other wrongful act. *Compare* CONSEQUENTIAL DAMAGES *and* INCIDENTAL DAMAGES.

Due process *See* SUBSTANTIVE DUE PROCESS *and* PROCEDURAL DUE PROCESS.

Duress A defense that applies when the defendant acts illegally and against his own will as a result of another's *unlawful threat* of bodily harm. Duress excuses an actor from the legal effects of his actions (*e.g.*, a defendant is not guilty for a theft committed under duress).

E

Earnout Contractual pricing provision in mergers and acquisitions stating that the seller of a business is to obtain additional future compensation based on the business achieving certain financial goals following the merger or acquisition.

Easement The right to use part of land owned by another for a special purpose. *See* EASEMENT APPURTENANT and EASEMENT IN GROSS.

Easement appurtenant An easement that benefits the grantee's (dominant tenant) land. When there is an easement appurtenant, there are *both dominant* and *servient tenements*. *Compare* EASEMENT IN GROSS.

Easement in gross An easement that does not benefit the grantee's land. Although there is a servient estate, but there is no *dominant estate*. *Compare* EASEMENT APPURTENANT.

Equitable servitude Covenants restricting the use of land that run with the land at equity and thus offer remedies at equity (*e.g.*, injunctions). *Compare* REAL COVENANTS.

Equity Set of legal principles that grant judges flexibility when applying the strict letter of the law, when such application leads to harsh results. The purpose of equity is to ensure that the application of the law leads to fair results.

Escrow Contractual arrangement in which a third party escrow service receives and disburses funds or other assets for the primary transacting parties, with the disbursement dependent on the consummation of a transaction and conditions agreed to by the transacting parties.

Executory contract Contract not yet been performed or executed by either side, such that failure to perform the contract by either side would constitute a breach of contract.

Executory period In a land sale contract, the period between the formation of the sale contract and the closing.

***Ex post facto* law** (Lat., a law "after the fact"). A law that does any of the following retroactively: (i) makes conduct criminal; (ii) establishes a stricter punishment for a crime; or (iii) alters the procedural or evidentiary rules in favor of the prosecution.

Extracontractual obligations Obligations outside of the explicit provisions of a contract that are imposed on a party.

F

False pretenses A specific intent crime consisting of the acquiring of title to the property of another through making false statements or misrepresentations with the intent of defrauding the owner.

False swearing Making a false statement under oath or equivalent affirmation, or swearing or affirming the truth of such a statement previously made, without believing the statement to be true.

First degree murder Under the modern statutory approach to murder, first degree murder is generally defined as all forms of murder having malic aforethought *and* premediation and deliberation. *Compare* SECOND DEGREE MURDER.

Force majeure Extraordinary and compelling unforeseen event or circumstance, such as a war, riot, crime, or "acts of God" (e.g., earthquake, flood), beyond the control of a party.

A party that is unable to fulfill the terms of a contract due to *force majeure* is excused from performance.

Freehold estate An estate where the possessor is the owner of the property (at least for a temporary period of time).

G

Grand theft The commission of LARCENY when the value of the property unlawfully taken exceeds some predetermined amount.

H

Habeas corpus Legal proceeding where a writ is brought to determine whether a person is being lawfully detained.

Heads of agreement *See* HEADS OF TERMS.

Heads of terms Set of agreed principles that precede and set forth the roadmap for the signing of a negotiated contract. They set out the basis of the deal in broad terms and normally include the obligation of the parties to work together in good faith to conclude a later, definitive agreement that sets for all material terms of the deal in detail. *Also known as* HEADS OF AGREEMENT.

Holdover tenant A tenant who keeps possession of the property beyond the expiration of the lease.

Homestead exemption Legal regime designed to protect the value of the homes from property taxes, creditors, and circumstances arising from the death of the homeowner spouse. Homestead exemptions have been enacted by the laws or constitutions of several US states.

I

Implied easement by prior use An easement that comes into being when an owner of two parcels of land uses one of them, the servient estate, to benefit the other in such a way that when he sells one of them, the purchaser can *reasonably expect* that the servient estate will continue to be used in a way that is consistent with its prior use.

In-court identification Modality of identification where an attorney asks a witness if she recognizes the perpetrator of a crime in court.

Incidental damages Legal damages for a loss generally arising out of breach of contract for commercially reasonable expenses, such as shipping or restocking or expenses reasonably associated with the resale of goods. *Compare* CONSEQUENTIAL DAMAGES *and* DIRECT DAMAGES.

Indictment Since a defendant may not cross-examine witnesses presented against him in a grand jury indictment, the Confrontation Clause does no apply. Compare RELIMINARY HEARING.

Indirect damages *See* CONSEQUENTIAL DAMAGES.

Infant A person who has not yet reached the legal age of majority (generally, eighteen years of age); a minor.

Intent (torts) The *mens rea* element for intentional torts, which is formed when the defendant possesses either: (i) purpose (a wanting or desiring) that a certain result come about; or (ii) knowledge to a substantial certainty that a result is substantially certain to come about as a result of his act (based on belief or knowledge).

Intervening cause An act that intervenes in the series of events after an act, such that it alters the resulting consequence. When intervening causes are strong enough to relieve wrongdoer of liability, they become SUPERSEDING CAUSES.

Involuntary manslaughter An *unintentional* killing lacking malice aforethought committed either with criminal negligence or during the commission of an unlawful act.

Issue preclusion *See* COLLATERAL ESTOPPEL.

J

Joinder The uniting of distinct claims or parties in an action.

Joint and several liability Liability in which each member of a group is responsible for the full payment of a judgment, debt, or other obligation of any other member of the group, leaving the members of the group to sort out the respective portions of the debt. Thus, with JOINT AND SEVERAL LIABILITY, if a creditor sues and recovers money from one partner, that partner may pursue the other partners for their respective share of obligation. This is a key difference between JOINT LIABILITY and JOINT AND SEVERAL LIABILITY; in joint liability, all joint debtors or defendants must be named in a law suit. *Compare* JOINT LIABILITY and SEVERAL LIABILITY.

Joint liability Liability of two or more persons (*e.g.*, spouses) for the full amount of a particular judgment, debt, or other obligation. Unlike with JOINT AND SEVERAL LIABILITY, JOINT LIABILITY, all joint debtors or defendants must be named in a law suit. *Compare* SEVERAL LIABILITY and JOINT AND SEVERAL LIABILITY.

K

Knowledge to a substantial certainty (torts) Knowledge of an extremely high risk that a particular consequence will materialize as a result of one's act. It may be based on knowledge or belief and, like purpose, satisfies the *mens rea* required in intentional torts.

L

Larceny A specific intent crime consisting of the unlawful taking and carrying away of the property of another with the intent to permanently deprive him thereof.

Leasehold estate An estate where the possessor is not the owner of the property (*e.g.*, in the case of a rental property). Possession will spring back to the owner after the current possessor's lease or rental comes to a close.

Letter of credit Written commitment issued by a bank guaranteeing that a seller will receive payment in full as long as certain delivery conditions have been fulfilled by the seller. The bank pays the outstanding amount in the event that the buyer fails to make payment on the purchase. *Compare* BANK GUARANTEE.

Libel A tort consisting of DEFAMATION that can be seen, such as a writing, printing, movie or statue and that harms a reputation, decreases respect, regard or confidence or induces disparaging, hostile or disagreeable opinions or feelings against an individual or entity. *Compare* SLANDER.

License (property law) A right to use another's property that is terminable at the will of the possessor of the land.

Liquidated damages clause See STIPULATED DAMAGES CLAUSE.

Longstop date Last date by which a contractual condition or set of conditions must be performed. Contracts normally contain consequences if the longstop date is not complied with (*e.g.*, if duty is not performed prior to a longstop date, the counterparty's duties are discharged).

M

Malum in se (Lat., "a wrong in itself"). An inherently evil or immoral act, regardless of whether it is prohibited.

Malum prohibitum (Lat., "a prohibited wrong"). An act or offense which is prohibited but is not inherently wrong (*e.g.*, failing to stop at a stop sign).

Merchantable title Title not subject to such reasonable doubt that it would create a just apprehension of its validity in the mind of a reasonable prudent person. Merchantable title is not necessarily good title; it may have *slight defects*.

Moral damages Damages awarded by courts to compensate for and alleviate the mental anguish, anxiety, damaged reputation, wounded feelings, moral shock, social humiliation, related physical suffering, and similar harm unjustly caused to a person. MORAL DAMAGES are meant to be compensatory rather than punitive in nature and purpose. They are most frequently seen within the context of DEFAMATION cases.

Mortgage Security for a debt given by a mortgagor (a debtor) to a mortgagee (a creditor) to secure a loan given to the mortgagor, usually for the purpose of purchasing land or some other real estate.

Mortgagee In a mortgage, the creditor, loan company, or bank that lends to the debtor, or mortgagor.

Mortgagor In a mortgage, the party that borrows from a creditor, loan company, or bank; a debtor.

N

Negligence *per se* Negligence established as a matter of law such that the plaintiff need not establish duty and breach. The violation of civil and criminal statutes gives rise to negligence *per se* in most states, such that the jury is instructed that the violation of a statute constitutes the breach of duty for the purposes of negligence.

Negotiable instrument Document guaranteeing an unconditional promise to pay a specific amount of money, either on demand, or at a specific time. Governed by Article 3 of the UCC, which includes PROMISSORY NOTES and BILLS OF EXCHANGE, but not LETTERS OF CREDIT, which are governed by UCC Article 4.

Nonjusticiable political question A question that involves the exercise of *discretionary power* by either the Legislative or the Executive Branch; it does not involve a *judicial* question to be decided by the judiciary.

Nuisance A condition or activity on another's land that unreasonably affects the other's right to enjoy and use his land. The standard is one of a person of *ordinary sensibility*.

O

Option contract Agreement between a purchaser and seller that gives the purchaser of the option the right to buy or sell real or personal property at a later date at an agreed upon price.

Ordinary majority *See* Simple majority.

Order to show cause Court order that requires one or more of the parties to justify, explain, or prove something to the court. They are commonly used when a judge needs more information before deciding whether or not to issue an order requested by a party.

P

Parol evidence Oral or written evidence of a bargain that occurred before the final terms of the contract were laid down and that was not made part of the final contract.

Parol evidence rule Rule of substantive law that states that supplementary oral or written evidence of any agreement prior to or contemporaneous with the laying down of the final terms of the contract cannot be used to contradict or vary the final agreement.

Partial-birth abortion Any abortion where a physician partially induces a vaginal delivery of the fetus prior to destroying and delivering the fetus.

Pendent parties jurisdiction The jurisdiction to adjudicate a claim against a party who is not otherwise within court's jurisdiction, because the claim by or against that party arises from the same core facts of another claim that is properly before the court.

Perfection Completion of steps required to be taken after the creation of a valid security interest in order to enforce it against third parties or the grantor in the event of his default.

Perjury Knowingly making a false statement under oath during an official proceeding, such as a trial or a grand jury hearing. For a statement to rise to the level of perjury in most states, it must be "material" to the proceeding, meaning that the false information could have affected the outcome of the proceeding.

Personalty Personal property, which is moveable, as contrasted with Realty (real property).

Photographic lineup Modality of identification where a witness identifies one suspect among others in a spread of photographs.

Pleading Documents filed by a litigant that set forth the material facts and legal arguments of his claims or defenses.

Police lineup Modality of identification in which suspects are lined up at a police station and a witness is asked if he recognizes the perpetrator among them.

Preliminary hearing Permits a defendant to cross-examine witnesses presented against him. Compare INDICTMENT.

Prevention principle Principle whereby a party may not enforce a contractual obligation against another party where it has prevented the other party from performing that obligation, aligned with the concept that no party may benefit from its own breach of contract.

Prima facie case A case in which the plaintiff presents sufficient evidence "on its first appearance" (Lat.) supporting the cause of action. If no contrary or rebutting evidence is presented, the plaintiff is entitled to a decision in his favor.

Privity of contract Doctrine whereby a contract cannot confer rights or impose obligations arising under it on any person or agent except the parties to it. Horizontal privity occurs when the benefits of a contract are given to a third party. Vertical privity arises when one of the parties to a contract enters into a contract with a third party.

Procedural due process One of the modalities of DUE PROCESS (the other being SUBSTANTIVE DUE PROCESS) consisting of the constitutional guarantees of notice and a hearing.

Profit à prendre An easement that grants the right to enter and remove timber, minerals, oil, gas, game, and other substances from another's land.

Promissory note Negotiable instrument where the issuer makes an unconditional promise in writing to pay a determined sum of money to a payee, either at a fixed or determinable future time or on demand of the payee, under specific terms. Regulated by the Convention Providing a Uniform Law for Bills of Exchange and Promissory Notes.

Proximate cause is legal causation that serves as a limitation on actual cause. The law limits those acts that are said to be "causes" of some consequence, requiring the acts to be related to the consequence through some foreseeable sequence of events. If an act is foreseeably related, it is said to be the proximate. Compare CAUSATION IN FACT.

Q

Qualified majority A majority requiring more votes or other conditions than a SIMPLE MAJORITY. It may, for example, require the votes of at least two thirds of the eligible voters or a limit on the number of abstentions that would be allowed in order for a measure to be adopted. *Also known as* SPECIAL MAJORITY. *Compare* SIMPLE MAJORITY *and* ABSOLUTE MAJORITY.

Quantum meruit A Latin expression meaning "as much as he deserves." This is a doctrine at equity that allows a party to recover for the value of the labor or materials delivered to another, even if there was no actual contract or if there was a contract and the party breached it, in order to prevent the other party's unjust enrichment.

R

Rape Under the common law, rape was defined as "the carnal knowledge of a woman forcibly and against her will." The modern law has departed from this view by defining rape in gender-neutral terms.

Ratione soli **doctrine** Under this doctrine, the owner of the soil *is the first occupant* and owner of whatever is found on the soil, including minerals and *ferae naturae*, regardless of who the finder is. Also known as THE "*AD COELUM* MINOR DOCTRINE."

Real covenant A promise relating to land use that runs with the land at law and is enforceable at law (offering monetary damages as remedies) between the original covenanting parties as a contract. Compare EQUITABLE SERVITUDE.

Realty Real property, which is immovable and fixed to the ground (*e.g.*, buildings, land), as contrasted with PERSONALTY.

Recklessness (torts) The purposeful disregard of a high probability of a resulting consequence (*e.g.*, of resulting emotional distress, in the case of the intentional infliction of emotional distress).

Remand Court procedure in which an appellate court sends back a case to a trial court or lower appellate court for further action.

Replevin An action at common law to recover *the possession* of personalty wrongfully taken from the plaintiff. Compare TROVER.

Replevy To exercise the common law action of REPLEVIN.

Res ipsa loquitur A negligence circumstantial evidence doctrine that is invoked when the facts create such a strong presumption of negligence that "the thing speaks for itself" (Lat.). The plaintiff is not required to introduce direct evidence.

Res judicata Under the doctrine of *res judicata* (Lat., the "the thing already adjudicated"), a party *may not litigate **claims*** that he raised or could have raised in a previous suit that reached a final judgment. *Also known as* CLAIM PRECLUSION.

Respondeat superior (Lat., "let the superior answer") The doctrine that a master or principal is *vicariously liable* for the negligence of his servants or agents, even when he was not himself negligent. This doctrine usually refers to the liability of employers for their employees.

Restitution Restoration of an original situation before an injury was caused, often in the form of repayment to the offended. In contract law, it puts the ***promisor*** back into the position that he would have been in had there been no contract.

Restrictive covenant (i) Provision in a deed limiting the use of the property and prohibiting certain uses; (ii) contractual clause of employment prohibiting a contracting party from engaging in similar employment for a specified period of time within a certain geographical area.

Right of first refusal Contractual right of a person or entity to be given the opportunity to enter into a transaction with the owner of something according to specified terms before the owner may enter into such a transaction with anyone else.

Robbery The specific intent crime that consists of the unlawful taking of property from another person or in the person's presence by the use of force or by threatening the imminent use of force.

S

Satisfaction Satisfactory fulfillment of a debt obligation through the rendering of an agreed-to lesser performance. *Compare* ACCORD.

Second degree murder Under the modern statutory approach to murder, second degree murder is generally defined as all forms of murder having malice aforethought, but, unlike FIRST DEGREE MURDER, lacks premeditation and deliberation (*e.g.*, depraved heart murder, felony murder committed in tandem with a non-inherently dangerous felony, etc.).

Secured loan Loan in which the borrower pledges some asset as collateral for the loan, which then becomes a secured debt owed to the creditor. The debt is thus secured against the collateral. If the borrower defaults, the creditor may take possession of the collateral. An unsecured debt, in contrast, is not connected to any specific piece of property; the creditor may only satisfy the debt against the borrower rather than the borrower's collateral and the borrower.

Several liability Liability of two or more persons for their own respective portions of a shared debt. *Compare* JOINT LIABILITY and JOINT AND SEVERAL LIABILITY.

Shelter principle Under this principle, if a possessor of some chattel or other property became the legitimate owner of the property under some theory of ownership (*e.g.*, adverse possession, accession, etc.), then all subsequent possessors may claim that good title was also passed to them if they legitimately acquired the good.

Showup Modality of identification in which police seize a suspect, bring him to the victim of a crime, and ask the witness if the suspect is the perpetrator. A showup usually occurs before an indictment, when time is of the essence.

Simple majority A majority consisting of more votes in favor than votes against, or, stated in another way, more "yea's" than "nay's," not withstanding the number of abstentions or voters absent. *Also known as* ORDINARY MAJORITY. *Compare* ABSOLUTE MAJORITY and QUALIFIED MAJORITY.

Slander A tort consisting of DEFAMATION that is spoken and heard and that harms a reputation, decreases respect, regard or confidence or induces disparaging, hostile or disagreeable opinions or feelings against an individual or entity. *Compare* LIBEL.

Solicitation The act of entreating, imploring, inducing, or encouraging another person to engage in some unlawful behavior.

Special damages *See* CONSEQUENTIAL DAMAGES.

Special majority *See* QUALIFIED MAJORITY.

Stare decisis (Lat., *Stare decisis et non quieta movere*: "to stand by decisions and not disturb the undisturbed") Legal principle by which judges are required to abide by precedents established in prior cases.

Statute of limitations Statute that sets the maximum time after an event in which legal proceedings based on that event may commence.

Stipulated damages clause A contractual clause that compensates losses of profits caused by breach, as calculated at the time of contracting. If a stipulated damages clause is upheld by a court, the amount of damages is not litigated in court. *Also known as* LIQUIDATED DAMAGES CLAUSE.

Sua sponte By order of the court or other authority "of its own will" (Lat.), without prompting by any third party.

Sublease A transfer of property that grants possession of the land to a new tenant for *part of the duration of a lease period*, even if it is as little as one minute. Compare ASSIGNMENT.

Subpoena Writ issued by court authority to compel the attendance of a witness at a judicial proceeding; disobedience may be punishable as a contempt of court.

Subrogation Legal situation created when one party takes over the rights or remedies of another against a third party. Subrogation may arise automatically as a matter of law or by contract, as is the case of contracts of insurance.

Substantive due process One of the modalities of DUE PROCESS (the other being PROCEDURAL DUE PROCESS) generally held to consist of unenumerated historical rights based on longstanding traditions.

Suicide pact An agreement whereby two or more people agree to kill one another.

Superseding cause An INTERVENING CAUSE that is strong enough to relieve a wrongdoer of liability.

Supplemental jurisdiction The jurisdiction that a court has over a claim that is *part of the same case or controversy* as another claim over which the court has *original jurisdiction*.

T

Time at large Situation where there is no identified completion deadline. Time is said to be at large when no contractual provision fixes a completion deadline or, where such a deadline is stipulated, the development of events (*e.g.*, requiring a contractor to complete works additional to those in the contract) and the operation of law negate the deadline. When time is at large, the contractor is only required to complete the works within a reasonable period of time. Time at large often arises in the application of liquidated damages in construction contracts. If time is at large, then it can be argued that liquidated damages cannot be applied, because there is no deadline from which liquidated damages can be calculated.

Tort A civil wrong, other than a breach of contract, for which the law provides a remedy.

Tortfeasor A person who has committed a tort.

Tortious interference An intentional tort that occurs when a person intentionally damages the plaintiff's contracts or business relationships. A typical example of tortious interference of contract is when a person commits a tort to come in between two parties' mutual contract. A typical example of tortious interference with business relationships is when a person makes false claims or accusations in order to drive business away from a person or company. *Also known as* INTENTIONAL INTERFERENCE WITH CONTRACTUAL RELATIONS.

Trover A remedy that allows the rightful owner of property to recover possession or to recover damages for the wrongful taking of his property. Compare REPLEVIN.

V

Voidable title Title that is fraudulently transferred or transferred through the owner's negligence. Although it is imperfect, it has the potential of becoming full title (if transferred to a *bona fide* purchaser, for example). Compare VOID TITLE.

Void Title Fatally flawed title that no action can cure or transform into full title. Compare VOIDABLE TITLE.

Voir Dire Judicial procedure in which attorneys examine prospective jurors to determine competency and potential bias. The process leads to the rejection or selection of those who will ultimately serve on the jury in a particular case.

Voluntary manslaughter An intentional killing mitigated by provocation in the heat of passion or other circumstances that negate malice aforethought.

W

Without prejudice Without any loss or waiver of rights or privileges. When used in negotiations, statements "without prejudice" cannot be used as evidence in court, since they are made for the purpose of settlement and not as concessions for litigation. When a lawsuit is dismissed without prejudice, none of the rights or privileges of the defendant are considered lost or waived, and if the defendant is later retried, he cannot invoke the doctrine of *res judicata*.